I0490897

THE ART OF GROWING RICH

Possible Practical steps on Thinking and Growing Rich

Michael Ellis

<u>LIVING RICH</u>

BALANCING WEALTH AND HAPPINESS
ESTATE PLANNING AND PHILANTHROPY

INTRODUCTION

The Art of Growing Rich is a comprehensive guide to building wealth and creating financial abundance. Are you fed up with living paycheck to paycheck, struggling to make ends meet, and constantly worrying about money? Do you dream of financial stability, security, and the freedom to live freely on your own terms? The book is designed to help readers develop a rich mindset, build a strong financial foundation, make wise investment decisions, and live a rich and fulfilling life. Either you are just starting out on your wealth-building journey or are looking to improve your financial situation, this book is an invaluable resource.

Wealth has been a coveted goal for generations, but it's often misunderstood. Many believe that being rich is solely about having a high income or a large bank account, but true wealth is much more than that. It's about having financial stability, security, and the liberty to live life on your own terms. In this book, we explore the psychology of wealth, the role of mindset in shaping your financial future, and the importance of having a wealth mindset.

The book begins by examining the psychology of wealth and abundance and the role of mindset in shaping our financial futures. We delve into the differences between being rich and appearing rich, and highlight the importance of having a wealth mindset. From there, we move on to building a strong financial foundation, including tips for budgeting, saving, reducing debt, and increasing earning potential.

We explore the world of investment and offer guidance on making wise investment decisions. We examine different investment options, evaluate opportunities, and provide strategies for minimizing risk. The book also covers portfolio management, tax planning, and the importance of diversification for long-term success.

In "The Art of Growing Rich," you will learn how to build a strong financial foundation, make wise investment decisions, minimize risk, and live a rich life. Imagine having the financial freedom to do what you want, when you want, without worrying about money. Imagine having the security of knowing that you have enough saved to live comfortably in your golden years. Imagine the peace of mind that comes from having a diversified portfolio and a plan in place for the future. With our step-by-step guide, you will be on your way to creating wealth and financial stability. Don't wait, start your journey towards financial freedom today by reading "The Art of Growing Rich."

CHAPTER ONE

WEALTH MINDSET
"Abundance Begins in the Mind" – Deepak Chopra

A positive mindset and wealth go hand in hand. Developing a wealthy mindset can help attract and maintain wealth in one's life, and wealth can help cultivate a positive mindset.

A positive mindset focuses on abundance and opportunities, allowing individuals to see the world through a lens of potential and possibility. This abundance mentality can increase confidence and decision-making skills, enabling individuals to make smart financial choices and investments. Additionally, a positive mindset helps individuals overcome obstacles, remain resilient, and consistent in the face of challenges. This resilience is critical in building and growing wealth over time.

Moreover, a positive mindset can attract what one desires, including wealth, into their lives through the power of manifestation. By focusing on positive thoughts and feelings, individuals can create a reality that aligns with their goals and aspirations.

Note that a positive mindset can cultivate gratitude and generosity, which can help individuals attract and retain wealth, and create a more fulfilling life. Wealth is not just about material possession, it is also about living a rich and meaningful life. By cultivating a positive mindset and a wealthy perspective, individuals can live a life that is abundant in all aspects.

PSYCHOLOGY OF ABUNDANCE

The psychology of abundance refers to the beliefs and attitudes that people hold about wealth, prosperity, and financial success. It encompasses the mental and emotional aspects of attracting, creating, and maintaining wealth in one's life.

People who have a wealth mindset believe that abundance is possible and achievable, and they view money and wealth as a positive and necessary aspect of life. They focus on growth, opportunity, and abundance, and they believe that they have the power to create their own financial success. On the other hand, those who have a scarcity mindset believe that there is not enough money, resources, or opportunities to go around, and they focus on lack, limitations, and competition.

To cultivate a wealth mindset, individuals can adopt several key attitudes and behaviors, such as:

Gratitude*:* Gratitude is the practice of appreciating and giving thanks for what one has, rather than focusing on what one lacks. When it comes to *The Art of Growing Rich*, gratitude plays a crucial role in shaping one's wealth mindset and attracting abundance into their life.

8

Think of gratitude as the fertile soil in which the seed of abundance can grow. Just as a garden cannot flourish without nourishment and care, our financial well-being cannot thrive without a foundation of gratitude. When we cultivate an attitude of gratitude, we pay attention to what we have, rather than what we don't have, and this shifts our perspective from scarcity to abundance.

Gratitude helps us recognize and appreciate the abundance that already exists in our lives, and it attracts more positive energy and opportunities. By focusing on the what we're grateful for, we're able to let go of negativity, stress, and fear, and instead cultivate a positive and optimistic outlook on life.

Gratitude is an essential component of the art of growing rich. It helps individuals cultivate a wealth mindset and attract abundance into their lives. By focusing on what they have and giving thanks for it, they set the stage for financial success and prosperity.

Mindfulness*:* Mindfulness is a situation where you focus your attention on the present, without judgment or distraction. When it comes to the *Art of Growing Rich,* mindfulness is a powerful tool for helping individuals cultivate a wealth mindset and achieve financial success.

Think of mindfulness as the canvas upon which the masterpiece of financial abundance is painted. It provides the foundation and clarity of thought needed to create and sustain wealth. Just as an artist must be fully present and focused in order to bring their vision to life, so must the individual seeking financial abundance be mindful in order to bring their wealth goals to fruition.

By being mindful, individuals can tap into their inner wisdom and creativity, which are crucial for making smart financial decisions and finding new opportunities. Mindfulness helps individuals avoid distractions, overcome limiting beliefs, and maintain a positive outlook even in the face of challenges. It allows them to focus on what they want to achieve and remain motivated and driven towards their financial goals.

In short, mindfulness is a key ingredient in the recipe for financial success. By incorporating it into their daily routine, individuals can cultivate a wealth mindset, make smart financial decisions, and live a life of abundance and prosperity.

Visualization: Visualization is a powerful tool for the mind and can be used to achieve wealth and financial success. It involves using the imagination to create vivid mental images of oneself in a desired state, such as being financially abundant. By visualizing a future state of prosperity and abundance, an individual can create an emotional connection to their goals and increase their motivation to pursue them.

Visualization can be compared to planting a seed in fertile soil. Just as a seed needs the right environment to grow and flourish, visualization provides the mind with a fertile environment to grow and manifest one's desired financial state. By regularly visualizing oneself as financially successful, an individual can cultivate the wealth mindset and attract abundance into their life.

In the same way that a gardener tends to their plants, nurturing them with sunlight, water, and care, one must tend to their visualization by regularly focusing on their desired state of abundance and nurturing it with positive thoughts, emotions, and actions.

The art of growing rich requires visualization as a key ingredient, just as a gardener must tend to their plants in order to reap a bountiful harvest. By regularly visualizing and tending to their desired financial state, individuals can cultivate the wealth mindset and reap the harvest of abundance in their lives.

Education: Education can be seen as the cornerstone of "The Art of Growing Rich." Just as an artist must continuously hone their skills and knowledge to perfect their craft, those who seek financial prosperity must continually educate themselves about personal finance, wealth creation, and investment strategies. By expanding their knowledge and understanding, individuals can make informed decisions, overcome financial challenges, and achieve their financial goals.

Think of education as the paintbrush in the hands of the artist, giving them the tools to create their masterpiece. Similarly, education equips individuals with the tools they need to build and maintain wealth, creating their own financial masterpiece.

Investing in personal finance education is like investing in high-quality art supplies. The more you act, the more you can create, and the greater your wealth will become. With education as your guide, you can navigate the complex financial world with ease, and you will be able to see opportunities for growth and abundance where others see obstacles and limitations.

Affirmations: Affirmations are hopeful statements that are repeated to oneself, usually as a form of self-encouragement and motivation. They can be a powerful tool in shaping one's beliefs, attitudes, and actions, and they can help cultivate a wealth mindset.

In relation to the title "The Art of Growing Rich," affirmations can be viewed as "seed statements" that are planted in the mind and watered with focus and belief. Just as a seedling needs the right conditions to grow into a healthy and productive plant, affirmations require repetition and positive reinforcement to take root in the mind and yield positive results in one's life.

For example, an affirmation related to the psychology of abundance might be: "I am worthy and deserving of wealth and financial prosperity." This statement plants the seed of abundance in the mind and helps individuals focus on their worth and potential to attract wealth into their lives. When repeated regularly, it can become a powerful belief that drives actions and decisions, leading to financial success and growth.

Adopting a wealth mindset can have a profound impact on a person's financial situation and well-being. It helps individuals focus on abundance, opportunities, and growth, and it gives them the confidence and motivation to pursue their financial goals. By changing their beliefs and attitudes about wealth, they can create a more abundant and prosperous life.

RICH HABITS AND BELIEFS

Rich Habits and Beliefs are a critical aspect of financial success and should be incorporated into any comprehensive guide on wealth building. In this context, a detailed analysis of these habits and beliefs can be presented as follows:

Saving and Investing*:* Establishing a savings and investment strategy is a crucial aspect of wealth building. By regularly setting aside a portion of their income and investing in appreciating assets, individuals can harness the power of compound interest and make their money work for them.

Responsibility and Accountability*:* Taking responsibility for one's financial situation and being accountable for spending and investment decisions are key components of wealth building. By being proactive and in control of their finances, individuals can ensure their financial success.

Continuous Education*:* Staying up-to-date with the latest finance and investment strategies is essential for wealth building. Regular education and self-improvement can provide individuals with the knowledge and tools needed to make informed decisions and achieve their financial goals.

Delayed Gratification*:* Building wealth takes time and requires discipline and sacrifice. However, by delaying immediate gratification and focusing on long-term gains, individuals can achieve financial stability and security.

Networking: Relationships are powerful and can play a significant role in wealth building. Building a strong network of successful individuals can provide individuals with new opportunities and insights into the financial world.

Positive Mindset: Having a positive and optimistic outlook on life, including finances, is an important component of wealth building. Believing in one's ability to achieve financial goals and embracing calculated risks can lead to greater financial success.

Incorporating "Rich Habits and Beliefs" into one's wealth-building strategy can provide individuals with the tools and mindset they need to achieve financial stability and security. While every journey to wealth is unique, adopting these habits and beliefs is a great starting point. With the right mindset and approach, individuals can unlock their financial potential and achieve their goals.

Wealth Mindset, explores the psychology of abundance and the beliefs and habits that are essential for creating wealth. The chapter discusses the importance of adopting a rich mindset and how this mindset can be developed through positive self-talk, visualization, and goal-setting. It also emphasizes the difference between being rich and appearing

CHAPTER TWO

FINANCIAL FOUNDATION

"Build a Strong Financial Foundation for Future Wealth" –
Warren Buffett

Financial foundation refers to the basic principles and practices of managing one's personal finances to build a stable and secure financial future. It is the foundation upon which an individual can build wealth, reduce debt, and achieve financial stability. A strong financial foundation involves developing and maintaining good habits, such as budgeting, saving, and reducing debt.

Budgeting is the act of coming up with a plan for how you will allocate and spend your income. This includes identifying your monthly expenses, such as rent, utilities, food, and transportation, and ensuring that your spending does not exceed your income. Saving is the practice of setting aside a portion of your income each month to reach financial goals, such as an emergency fund or a down payment on a home. Reducing debt involves paying off high-interest loans and credit card balances and avoiding new debt in the future.

Investment is another key component of financial foundation. Investment allows you to grow your wealth over time by taking advantage of opportunities in various financial markets, such as stocks, bonds, and real estate. However, it is crucial to understand the risks associated with investing money that you can afford to lose. It is also crucial to have a long-term investment strategy that commemorate with your financial goals and risk tolerance.

BUDGETING, SAVING, AND DEBT REDUCTION

In this comprehensive guide, we will cover the key aspects of budgeting, saving, and debt reduction. To start, it's important to track your spending for a month to gain a clear understanding of your financial habits. This will allow you to create an accurate budget by listing all your sources of income and expenses, including fixed expenses such as rent or mortgage, utilities, etc., variable expenses such as groceries, entertainment, etc., and discretionary expenses such as shopping, dining out, etc. By comparing your expenses to your income, you can determine if you have a surplus or deficit and make any necessary adjustments to balance your budget.

In terms of saving, automating your savings by setting up automatic transfers from your checking account to your savings account can be a powerful tool for building wealth. You can also maximize your returns by choosing a high-yield savings account. A solid emergency fund is crucial, so be sure to set aside money for unexpected expenses and make that a priority in your budget. Consider having multiple savings goals, such as short-term (vacation), medium-term (down payment on a house), and long-term (retirement), to ensure that you're saving for all your financial priorities. It's also important to avoid lifestyle inflation and stick to your budget, even as your income increases.

When it comes to debt reduction, start by creating a list of all your debts and their interest rates. Give priority to paying off high-interest debt first, such as credit card debt, to minimize the amount of interest you pay over time. If you have multiple debts with high-interest rates, debt consolidation may be an option worth exploring. By making more than the minimum payment on your debts, you can help pay off your debt faster and save on interest. Avoid taking on new debt while you're paying off existing debt to maintain your debt reduction progress. If you're having difficulty managing debt, alternative payment options such as a debt management plan or credit counseling may be worth considering.

INVESTMENT STRATEGY AND PORTFOLIO MANAGEMENT

Investing your money is an essential part of building wealth and securing your financial future. However, with so many investment opportunities available, it can be strenuous to know where to start and how to develop a successful investment strategy. This guide will direct you understand the basics of investment strategy and portfolio management, and provide you with the knowledge and tools you need to build a diversified and profitable portfolio.

Why Invest?

Investing your money is a proven way to grow your wealth over time. By investing in a variety of assets, such as stocks, bonds, and real estate, you can benefit from compound interest, which is the interest earned on your initial investment plus the interest earned on any previous interest earned. In other words, your money has the potential to grow faster when invested than when it is left in a savings account.

Creating an Investment Strategy

When developing your investment strategy, it's important to consider your long-term goals, risk tolerance, and time horizon. Do you want to save for a specific goal, such as retirement or a down payment on a house? How much risk are you willing to take on, and for how long? Answering these questions will help you determine your investment objectives and the types of investments that will best align with those goals.

Diversification is Key

Diversification is a fundamental principle of investment strategy and is key to reducing risk and maximizing returns. By investing in a mix of different assets, you can spread your risk and reduce the impact of any one investment on your overall portfolio. A well-diversified portfolio typically includes stocks, bonds, real estate, and commodities.

Portfolio Management

Once you have established your investment strategy and created a diversified portfolio, it's important to regularly monitor and manage your investments. This involves tracking your portfolio's performance, making adjustments as needed, and rebalancing your portfolio to ensure it remains in line with your investment goals.

Investment strategy and portfolio management are critical components of building wealth and securing your financial future. By taking the time to understand your investment goals, risk tolerance, and the importance of diversification, you can develop a successful investment strategy and create a well-balanced portfolio that will help you reach your financial goals. Whether you're a seasoned investor or just starting out, it's never too late to begin building your wealth through smart investing.

Financial Foundation, focuses on the practical aspects of wealth creation. The chapter covers budgeting and saving, reducing debt, and improving credit score. It also explores investment options and the importance of understanding one's risk tolerance. The chapter provides practical tips and strategies for increasing earning potential and building a strong financial

CHAPTER THREE

SMART INVESTMENTS

"Invest smart, not hard" – Warren Buffett

Investing your hard-earned money can be both exciting and nerve-wracking, especially when it comes to making smart investment decisions. The world of investments is filled with endless possibilities, but finding the right path to financial growth and stability can be a challenge. That's where smart investments come in - they offer a calculated and informed approach to investing that prioritizes both returns and risk management.

Picture a sailor setting sail on a sea of investments. The vast ocean presents endless opportunities for riches, but it's also filled with hidden dangers and treacherous waters. A smart sailor wouldn't set sail without a well thought-out plan, a map of the best route, and an understanding of the winds and currents. The same goes for smart investments. By taking the time to conduct thorough research and analysis, you can chart a course to financial success and ensure a steady return on your investment.

Smart investments aren't just about finding the next hot stock or trendy mutual fund. It's about considering your personal financial goals, risk tolerance, market trends, and inflation. With this information in hand, you can make informed decisions that lead to long-term growth and stability, helping you reach your financial destination with confidence. So why wait? Start charting your course to smart investments today and secure your financial future.

UNDERSTANDING INVESTMENT OPTIONS

Investing is a key component of building wealth and securing financial stability. However, with so many investment possibilities available, it can be strenuous to know where to start. Understanding the different types of investments and their unique characteristics is essential to making informed investment decisions.

Stocks*:* A stock denotes ownership in a company and allows you to participate in its growth and success. Stocks can be bought and sold on stock exchanges, and the value of a stock is determined by its current market price. Stocks can offer high potential returns, but they also come with higher level of risk.

Bonds*:* A bond is essentially a loan to a company or government. When you purchase a bond, you essentially loaning funds to the issuer and receiving periodic payment interests in return over a set period of time. Bonds are generally viewed as a lower-risk investment option compared to stocks, but they also tend to offer lower returns.

Real Estate: Real estate investment can take many forms, from investing in rental properties to participating in real estate investment trusts (REITs). Real estate investments can offer steady, long-term returns, but they can also be affected by factors such as property values, interest rates, and the state of the housing market.

Mutual Funds*:* Mutual funds involves participating in diverse range of investments including stocks, bonds, and other securities through a single investment vehicle that aggregates funds from numerous investors. By investing in a mutual fund, you could gain exposure to a variety of assets without having to purchase each one individually. Mutual funds are directed by professional fund managers who are responsible for making investment choices on behalf of the fund's stakeholders. There are different types of mutual funds, such as index funds, which track a specific market index, and actively managed funds, where the fund manager selects the securities in the fund's portfolio.

Exchange-Traded Funds (ETFs): ETFs are similar to mutual funds in that they offer exposure to a diverse portfolio of assets, but they trade like stocks on an exchange. ETFs can provide low-cost and convenient way to invest in a particular market or sector, such as technology or real estate.

Certificates of Deposit (CDs): CDs are a type of low-risk, fixed-income investment. When you invest in a CD, you agree to leave your money on deposit with a bank for a specified period of time, usually ranging from three months to five years. In exchange for your commitment, the bank pays a fixed interest rate on the deposit. CDs are considered to be a relatively safe investment option, but they generally offer lower returns compared to other investment options.

Savings Accounts: Savings accounts are a traditional investment option offered by banks and other financial institutions. They offer a low-risk way to save and earn a modest return in the form of interest. Savings accounts are FDIC-insured, meaning that your deposit is insured up to $250,000 per account.

However, there are many investment options available to meet different investment goals, risk tolerance, and time horizons. It is important to understand the characteristics and potential benefits and risks of each option before making an investment decision. A well-diversified investment portfolio that includes a mix of different types of investments can help manage risk and potentially increase returns over time.

MINIMIZING RISK AND MAXIMIZING RETURNS

Minimizing risk and maximizing returns is a crucial aspect of smart investing. This involves a balanced approach to investing that takes into account both the potential risks and rewards of a particular investment. The purpose is to find a balance between these two factors, resulting in a portfolio that has the potential for strong returns while minimizing the likelihood of significant losses.

To better understand the concept of minimizing risk and maximizing returns, let's take a closer look at some practical examples:

Diversification: Imagine you have invested all your money in a single stock, and that stock suddenly experiences a sharp decline. Your entire investment portfolio would suffer as a result. However, if you had diversified your investments across multiple stocks, the impact of a single stock performing poorly would be less severe. A practical way to diversify your investments, it is advisable to allocate funds in a combination of stocks, bonds, and real estate.

Asset Allocation: This strategy involves diversifying your investment portfolio by allocating funds among various asset categories, including equities, bonds, and property. Take for instance, a conservative investor may assign a larger portion of his portfolio to bonds and a smaller portion to stocks. If you are a more aggressive investor, you may assign a larger portion of your portfolio to stocks and a smaller portion to bonds. By having a balanced mix of these assets, you can minimize risk while still having the potential for strong returns.

Long-term investment horizon: Imagine you invested in a stock that experienced a temporary dip but went on to experience significant growth over the long term. If you had held onto the stock for the long term, you would have benefited from its growth. This is why a long-term investment horizon can be beneficial. By putting your money into long-term investments, you have the chance to reap the rewards of market growth in the future.

Investment in high-quality assets: Investing in high-quality assets, such as blue-chip stocks and investment-grade bonds, can help reduce the risk of significant losses. For example, if you invest in well-established companies with a strong track record, such as Apple or Johnson & Johnson, you can reduce the risk of losing money compared to investing in a less established company.

Monitoring and Rebalancing: Regular monitoring of your investments and periodic rebalancing of your portfolio can help ensure that it remains aligned with your risk tolerance and financial goals. For example, if you find that your portfolio is heavily invested in a single asset class, such as stocks, you may need to sell some stocks and invest in bonds to rebalance your portfolio.

Lastly, minimizing risk and maximizing returns is a critical aspect of smart investing. By using a balanced approach and incorporating strategies such as diversification, asset allocation, a long-term investment horizon, investment in high-quality assets, and monitoring and rebalancing, you can potentially reduce the risk of significant losses while still having the potential for strong returns. It's important to remember that there are no guarantees in the world of investing, and you should always anticipate the potential occurence of losses. However, by following a smart investment strategy, you can increase the likelihood of long-term financial success.

Smart Investments, is dedicated to the art of wise investment decisions. The chapter covers the different types of investment vehicles and options, including stocks, bonds, real estate, and alternative investments. It explains how to evaluate investment opportunities and minimize risk, and provides strategies for building a diversified portfolio that is aligned with one's

CHAPTER FOUR

LIVING RICH

"Live richly, give generously" - *Anonymous*

Living a rich life and avoiding economic turmoil are two important goals for many individuals. Financial stability and independence are essential for long-term happiness and peace of mind. However, achieving these goals can be challenging in today's rapidly changing economy. Economic downturns, job losses, and unexpected expenses can all disrupt financial stability, making it difficult to build wealth and avoid financial stress.

The key to avoiding economic turmoil and building wealth is to adopt smart financial practices and invest in a balanced and diversified portfolio. This requires a combination of budgeting, saving, and investing, as well as a strong understanding of financial markets and trends. It is also important to note potential risks and to make informed decisions when it comes to investments.

In order to achieve financial stability and live a rich life, it is crucial to have a long-term perspective and to adopt a disciplined and consistent approach to investing. This involves setting financial goals, creating a budget, and investing in a variety of assets such as stocks, bonds, and real estate. It is also important to stay informed and educated about economic trends and to seek professional advice when necessary.

Living a rich life and avoiding economic turmoil is achievable for anyone with the right combination of discipline, education, and smart financial practices. By following these principles and investing in a balanced and diversified portfolio, you can increase your chances of financial success and stability in the long run.

BALANCING WEALTH AND HAPPINESS

Balancing wealth and happiness are common challenges for many individuals, as the pursuit of financial success can often come at the cost of one's well-being and personal fulfillment. While wealth can bring a certain level of comfort and security, it does not necessarily lead to happiness. On the other hand, pursuing happiness at the expense of financial stability can also lead to stress and dissatisfaction. Achieving a healthy balance between wealth and happiness requires a deliberate and thoughtful approach to both personal and financial goals.

Here are some tips to help you balance wealth and happiness, along with practical examples to illustrate each point:

Set realistic financial goals: It is important to set achievable financial goals that align with your values and priorities. This can help you avoid overstressing about finances and make sure you are working towards something that brings you happiness and fulfillment. For example, if traveling and experiencing new cultures is important to you, set a goal to save enough money each year to take a trip.

Find a balance between work and leisure: Work is an important component of financial stability, but it is crucial to find a balance between work and leisure activities that bring you joy and relaxation. This can help you avoid burnout and increase overall happiness. For example, if you enjoy playing golf, make sure to schedule time each week to play a round or two, even if it means cutting back on work-related activities.

Spend money on experiences, not just things: Research has shown that spending money on experiences, such as travel or cultural events, brings more long-term happiness than buying material possessions. Instead of buying a new car or a large house, consider investing in experiences that will create lasting memories, such as a trip to Europe or a cooking class.

Invest in relationships: Strong relationships with family, friends, and loved ones are critical to overall happiness and well-being. Make time for the people you care about and invest in building meaningful relationships. For example, make plans to have dinner with friends once a week, or schedule a monthly video call with a family member who lives far away.

Give back to others: Giving to others, whether through charitable donations or volunteering, has been shown to bring a sense of purpose and fulfillment that contributes to overall happiness. For example, consider volunteering at a local soup kitchen or donating a portion of your income to a charity that aligns with your aspirations.

Prioritize self-care: Taking care of your psychological and physical well-being is essential to both happiness and financial stability. Make time for activities that nourish your well-being, such as exercise, meditation, or hobbies. For example, join a yoga or meditation class, or make a commitment to go for a walk each day, even if it's just for 15 minutes.

By following these tips and finding a balance between wealth and happiness, you can work towards achieving both financial stability and personal fulfillment. It is imperative to remember that the pursuit of wealth and happiness is a lifelong journey, and finding the right balance may require ongoing adjustments and self-reflection. For example, if you find out that you are allocating too much time at work and not enough time with friends and family, consider adjusting your work schedule to create more balance in your life. The key is to be proactive, intentional, and conscious about how you are spending your time and money, and to make adjustments as needed to ascertain that you are on track to achieve both wealth and happiness.

ESTATE PLANNING AND PHILANTHROPY

Estate Planning and Philanthropy are crucial components of a comprehensive financial plan that can help individuals achieve their personal and financial goals, as well as make a lasting impact on society.

I. Estate Planning

A. Definition and Purpose

Estate planning refers to the process of organizing, managing, and distributing an individual's assets after death. It involves creating a comprehensive plan that considers an individual's personal and financial goals, as well as tax implications, to ensure that their assets are distributed according to their wishes. Estate planning is important because it provides peace of mind and helps to minimize taxes, while also avoiding the lengthy and costly probate process.

B. Estate Planning Techniques

Wills and Trusts

A will is a legal document that outline how an individual's assets will be distributed after their death. Trusts, on the contrary, are legal entities that hold and manage assets for the benefit of designated beneficiaries. Wills and trusts can be used together to ensure that an individual's assets are distributed according to their wishes, while also minimizing taxes.

Powers of Attorney

The power of an attorney is a document that gives someone else the power of making decisions in your stead in the event that you become incapacitated. This can include financial, legal, and medical decisions, and it is important to choose someone who you believe to act in your best interests.

Advanced Healthcare Directives

Advanced healthcare directives, such as living wills, are documents that outline an individual's wishes for medical treatment in the event that they become unable to make their own decisions. These documents are an important part of estate planning because they can help ensure that an individual's medical treatment aligns with their personal values and beliefs.

C. Benefits of Estate Planning

Peace of Mind

Estate planning provides peace of mind, knowing that your assets will be distributed as you wish and that your loved ones will be taken care of in the event of your demise.

Avoiding Probate

Probate is a legal process that can be time-consuming and costly. Estate planning can help avoid probate by establishing a clear plan for distributing assets after death.

Minimizing Taxes

Estate planning can help minimize taxes by taking advantage of tax planning strategies, such as tax-deferred investment options and charitable giving. This can help ensure that more of your assets are passed on to your loved ones, rather than being lost to taxes.

II. Philanthropy

A. Definition and Purpose

Philanthropy refers to the act of giving money, time, or resources to support a good cause. It can take many forms, including charitable donations, volunteer work, or social investing. Philanthropy is important because it allows individuals to make a positive impact on society, while also providing personal satisfaction, tax benefits, and legacy building opportunities.

B. Types of Philanthropy

Charitable Giving

Charitable giving is the most common form of philanthropy, which involves making monetary donations to non-profit organizations. Charitable giving can be used to support causes that align with an individual's personal values and beliefs, and it can also provide tax benefits.

Volunteer Work

Volunteer work involves giving time and skills to support a cause. Volunteer work can be a rewarding way to make a difference in your community and it can also provide personal satisfaction.

Social Investing

Social investing involves making investment decisions based on social and environmental criteria, in addition to financial considerations. Social investing can be a way to align your investment portfolio with your personal values and beliefs, while also making a positive impact on society.

C. Benefits of Philanthropy

Personal Satisfaction

Philanthropy can provide a sense of personal satisfaction and fulfillment, knowing that one's resources are being used to make a positive impact on society.

Tax Benefits

Philanthropy can also offer tax benefits, as charitable donations may be tax-deductible.

Legacy Building

Philanthropy can help individuals build a legacy and make a lasting impact on the world, long after they have passed away.

Estate planning can provide peace of mind and minimize taxes, while philanthropy can provide personal satisfaction, tax benefits, and legacy building opportunities.

> Living Rich, focuses on the importance of balancing wealth and happiness. The chapter provides tips for maintaining a wealthy mindset and attitude, and for using wealth for good, such as philanthropy and estate planning. The chapter concludes by emphasizing the importance of living a rich and fulfilling life,

The topic of "The Art of Growing Rich" is an extensive guide to creating and maintaining financial prosperity. A wealth mindset is the foundation of this process, and it involves having a positive and growth-oriented attitude towards money, as well as an understanding of the role it plays in your life. This mindset is characterized by key traits such as determination, discipline, and a focus on long-term goals.

Building a strong financial foundation is also crucial in the journey to financial freedom. This involves developing a budget that allows you to live within your means, pay off debt, and build a back up fund for unexpected expenses. In addition, it is important to educate yourself on personal finance and understand key concepts such as saving, investing, and retirement planning.

Smart investments are a key component of the "Art of Growing Rich." This involves carefully researching and evaluating different investment opportunities, and making informed decisions that align with your financial goals. Whether it's stocks, bonds, real estate, or other assets, having a diverse portfolio and understanding the market can help you grow your wealth over time.

Finally, living a rich lifestyle is also an important aspect of "The Art of Growing Rich." This means enjoying the fruits of your labor, but also being mindful of your spending and not falling into the trap of living beyond your means. It's about finding a balance between saving and spending, and experiencing the joys of life without sacrificing your long-term financial goals.

www.ingramcontent.com/pod-product-compliance
Lightning Source LLC
Chambersburg PA
CBHW071145220526
45467CB00015B/1975